Praise for FATE:

The range of voices amongst this year's poetry entries was inspiring, by turns deeply personal, speaking clearly to lived experience, and alternately led by engagement with myth, fable, and other interpretations of *fate*.
Dagne Forrest, Award Winning Poet

This year's pool of poetry submissions varied greatly, with many unique and powerful voices commanding our attention.
Mason Nunemaker, Award Winning Poet

As a previous winner of the Poetry category, I was delighted to be asked to take part in this year's judging process. The entries were diverse and of an exceptional standard. It was a pleasure to read them.
Kitty Donnelly, Award Winning Poet

Other Publications:

Shakespeare In Debt
by Ted Stanley

Who's Afraid Of The Dark – Not Me!
by Sarah Smith

The Dog With The Head Transplant
by Julian Earl

Survival
Award Winning Short Stories

Survival
Award Winning Poetry

Stardust
Award Winning Short Stories

Stardust
Award Winning Poetry

Changes
Award Winning Short Stories

Changes
Award Winning Poetry

Fate
Award Winning Short Stories

FATE
Award Winning Poetry
Edited by Ted Stanley

FATE
AWARD WINNING POETRY

1st Edition published in the UK in 2024 by
Hammond House Publishing Ltd

ISBN: 978-1-7399985-9-2

The right of the individual writers to be identified as the author of this work has been asserted in accordance with sections 77 and 78 of the Copyright Designs and Patents act 1988.

All rights reserved. No part of this publication may be reproduced, stored in a retrieval system, or transmitted in any form or by any means, electronic, mechanical, photocopying, recording or otherwise, without the permission of the Publisher in writing.

Page Design by Alex Thompson
Proofreading by Debbie Adkins & Elis Ballard
Cover Design by Ted Stanley & Alex Thompson
Cover Image by Justin Fancourt

Cover image adapted from The Poet by Justin Fancourt. Produced by permission of the artist. All rights reserved.

The opinions expressed in this book are entirely those of the individual authors and are not endorsed or supported by the publishers or their sponsor, University Centre Grimsby.

Contains language that may be considered unsuitable for a younger audience.

Hammond House Publishing Ltd
13 Dudley Street, Grimsby,
Lincolnshire, DN31 2AE
United Kingdom

www.hammondhouse.org.uk

FATE
Award Winning Poetry

Enjoy this eclectic collection of poetry and song that brings together award-winning writers from around the world.

FATE is the eighth in a series of poetry anthologies, each featuring a different theme and including the winning and shortlisted entries from the annual *Hammond House International Literary Prize*.

Includes the winner of the
2023 International Literary Prize

The opinions expressed in this book are entirely those of the individual authors and are not endorsed or supported by the University Centre Grimsby.

Contents

Introduction • Ted Stanley xii

Award-Winning Poetry

The Purple Dress • Vasiliki Albedo, Greece 1

The Fugitive • Ronald Atilano, Australia 3

Aberdeen Street • Veronique Bequin, Canada 5

existential odyssey • Brooke Bolt, United States 7

One Day In Camden • Shirley Bunyan, United Kingdom 9

Magdalena • Jeanette Burney, United States 12

Scattering your ashes • Richard Burtle, United Kingdom 14

Catalina's Cattle • Jonathan Cant, Australia 16

Darius on the Underground • Alan Coombe, United Kingdom 18

Warnham Pond • Alan Coombe, United Kingdom 20

Creole Wedding • Jean Cooper Moran, United Kingdom 22

If the night had hands • Grace Copeland, United Kingdom 25

stopping the bleeding • Lucy Crispin, United Kingdom 27

Nostalgia is the Devil • Gillian D'Souza, Germany 30

The Opening • Hallie Denison, United States 32

Contents

An ill-fitting dress of somebody else's design • Steven Duggan, Ireland	34
Supermarketsweep • Steven Duggan, Ireland	35
Rare beauty • Kate Durrant, Ireland	36
Cauldron, Star • Elia Elton, Australia	39
The Chthonic Switchboard Blues • Deborah Finding, United Kingdom	40
American Psycho • Jacqueline Gamboa, United States	42
Phone Call • Jennifer Harrison, Australia	44
The Idea Of It • Amanda Huggins, United Kingdom	46
High Tide • Dave Kurley, Portugal	48
Washed Up • Donald McCrory, Spain	50
The Verdict • Donald McCrory, Spain	52
A Piece of Glass • Donald McCrory, Spain	54
Stormcock Harbinger • Alison McNulty, United Kingdom	56
Paternoster Row • Graeme Miles, Australia	58
Forever Walk • Alan Mitchell, United Kingdom	60
This Machine • Alan Mitchell, United Kingdom	62
Rite of Passage • Val Ormrod, United Kingdom	64

When Cassandra Stumbles • Miranda Pratt, United States	66
A Writer's Fate • Jean Rafferty, United Kingdom	68
Sad Outcomes • Gabhainn Ritchie, United Kingdom	69
The Lonely Prince • Angel Rodriguez, United States	70
Ma Mer, Maman • Paris Rosemont, Australia	71
Pleading • Paula Rowlands, Australia	73
A Kismet Path • Mervyn Seivwright, Germany	74
Conkers • Lee Slingsby, United Kingdom	76
Peregrine • Simon Tindale, United Kingdom	79
Bathing the Tyrant • Glen Wilson, United Kingdom	81
They Will be Winged • Raya Yarbrough, United States	84
Well Maybe Anyway, This Was destiny • Kathy Zwick, United Kingdom	86

Songwriting (Lyrics Category)

The Cloak • Michael Pettit, South Africa	92
Hey God, So What's The Hurry? • Jim Donaldson, United States	94
Over The Moon • Peter Ludgate, United Kingdom	96

Illustrations

Justin Fancourt	iii
Glynne Bulman	xiv
Trevor Bounford	1
Howard Halsall	3
Marzena Wilkes	14
Glynne Bulman	25
Trevor Bounford	27
Doriano Solinas	48
Fabio Sironi	81
Justin Fancourt	89
Justin Fancourt	90
Justin Fancourt	98

Acknowledgements

Thank you to: Elis Ballard, Alex Thompson, Dan Burks, Deborah Geddes, Debbie Adkins, Anjali Wierny, Leanne Doyle, Jonathon, Katherine and Freya Williams-Stanley, Richard and Rupert Hall.

And to the University Centre Grimsby for sponsoring the International Literary Prize and the National Lottery Community Fund for supporting our writers' groups.

Thank you to the competition judges: Kitty Donnelly, Dagne Forrest, Paul Sutherland, Mason Nunemaker, Kirily McKellor and Penelope McMorris.

Finally, thank you to all the writers who submitted such a wonderful collection of poems. We are sorry we were unable to include more.

And to the artists for their beautiful illustrations.

Competition Judges

Kitty Donnelly
Dagne Forrest
Paul Sutherland
Mason Nunemaker
Kirily McKellor
Penelope McMorris

Illustrators

Trevor Bounford
Glynne Bulman
Howard Halsall
Fabio Sironi
Doriano Solinas
Marzena Wilkes
Justin Fancourt

Introduction

Do we all travel on life's journey in one world, which we each perceive and experience differently, or is it our fate to live in parallel worlds, our experiences symbiotic but separate, shrouded in mystery from our fellow travellers but yearning to be seen and heard? Can we tap deep into the subconscious mind where the true meaning of our human experiences lies hidden, waiting to be to be born again in stories, poetry, theatre, film and song?

Perhaps the intrigue, humour, pathos and sometimes pain in this volume of precious poems will provide a rewarding glimpse into the world of others, or help us see our own world from a different perspective. They may not, in themselves, solve the problems of humankind but perhaps, in helping us understand each other better, pave the way for peaceful co-existence.

In the introduction to our 2022 anthology, *Stardust*, I suggested, somewhat controversially, that it was the storytellers, not the politicians, who hold the power for change and urged members of our literary community to 'Let your writing light the path to a brighter future'. I think recent events have made my case very well and maybe in future the postman won't always have to ring so many times in order to be heard.

Will it be fate that brings us to greater understanding of our fellow human beings or is it just a matter of time?

TED STANLEY

AWARD WINNING POETRY

"There's nowhere you can be that isn't where you're meant to be."

JOHN LENNON

The Purple Dress
Vasiliki Albedo
Greece

I entered my mother's bedroom
like crossing into the night.
It was July and the forbidden
plum dress shimmered

in her dark closet, heat haze
rising off tarmac. I unfastened
hooks from delicate eyelets
and tried it on, no longer myself

in the mirror. I never saw my mother
in that dress. Too deep, she said.
Not a colour that could disguise
pain— the colour of bruises

and cassocks. So much can fit
into a garment: the afternoon
when my mother ran to her father,
purple-faced in the clutch

of his final heart-attack.
The cigarette fug in the air.
It was her fourteenth birthday.
Blueberry trifle still stains her dress.

Highly Commended in the Poetry Category

The Fugitive
Ronald Atilano
Australia

It is only when our characters and events begin to disobey us that they begin to live. – John Fowles, 'The French Lieutenant's Woman'

I hear the slow tapping of his typewriter
As a distant carriage echoes and disappears,
Knowing that as my steps fall,
He's writing every kilometre of the avenue I walk on.
I see him on the face of the clocktower,
Observing the city he had constructed from words,
While an evening rain descends above the streetlights,
A rain of riddles and paradoxes,
Of palindromes pattering and eddying
Into the black sewers.

I stand in the middle of the bridge, hearing the neon-call
Of his ordinances and advertisements,
The omniscient eyes and hips of his billboards,
Supermarkets and movie-houses.
I see his verses posted on underpass walls,
Littered with certificates and fabricated names.

At the station, his armoured platoons congregate,
Constables of routes and signboards,
Waiting to take me to my appointed destination
And fate,
While out in the streets, I see my fellow phantoms
Being carted away down traffic lights
And tramways, imprisoned by wagons of rain.

And suddenly I've wandered into a hidden ghetto,
A shelter forgotten by his summoned storm,
Backstreet of crippled slumhouses, of black angels,
Magicians and marauders,
My newfound carnival of the fallen
And the lost.

Darkness wraps me in its wings
As his typewriter's carbonic shadows pursue me,
My footsteps disappearing in the mist—

Judges' Choice in the Poetry Category

Aberdeen Street
Veronique Bequin
Canada

I was lost in my neighbourhood
five blocks away from familiarity
on a sunny day at minus twenty

sunday morning light
where there had been none
for weeks
no one saw me when I read the sign

white on blue
a municipal Saltire
Aberdeen Street claimed
in a small town in southwestern Ontario
where everything's named

for only one kind of settler
white and male by birthright
I take notice

the street name is part of another story
from a time before the small Ontario town

from a place wedded to the North Sea
where I was waiting for assimilation
that never came

standing still long enough for once
to let go of what might have been
breathing out an accommodation of exiles

from the streets of Aberdeen
on the fifty-seventh parallel
to Aberdeen Street
on a sunny day at minus twenty.

SHORTLISTED IN THE POETRY CATEGORY

existential odyssey
BROOKE BOLT
United States

oh God i'm changing
metamorphosis, the sorceress, in search for Morpheus
a thousand voices in the choir inspired by the desire of
Orpheus
subliminal ecstasy, breaking the matrix meets greek legacy
Goddess of spring and the underworld
i am Persephone
pursuing the rest of me
my mind is not done growing yet
i shed my old self every time the sun sets
Dàeira, she who knows, i became this epithet
and i became again
and then once more
three times and then four
this is just the start
where i end and i begin are worlds apart
undress me by the centuries
sensory memories i feel the pain of previous civilizations'
injuries
in my mind's inquires of history, my ancestors and their
mysteries, the ruins of their victories
the process of spreading the ashes moved like molasses but

it covered the masses in black all the same
there is a secret hidden in my given name
speak it and it will leave cuts all over your tongue, it wasn't
meant to be learned by anyone
worshiping the paper of a blank page like it's a glass cage
made to hold words spoken by an all wise, powerful mage
when he tells of the start of a new age
i don't give much thought to prophecies, just more
hypotheses by oracle prodigies with promises of
commodities of quality or other worldly atrocities
evolution as a philosophy, i'm on an existential odyssey
if you can't keep up i make no apologies, i'm not trying to
end up like Socrates
modern minds manifesting into masters
masters of matter manipulation, writing new chapters into
structural fractures
creators of new patterns, beings born on the rings of Saturn
scattered , climbing celestial ladders to build a new Athens
stranger things happen, i've been flying on the backs of
dragons
speaking a language as dead as latin
you can't understand what i'm saying but i'm
praying, praying as my former self starts decaying
oh God i'm changing, i feel ancient
an angel bathing in its creation
an occasion complacent in its containment
only falling from heaven to make a statement
born again, i forgot i had to be somewhere
i'll meet myself there

One Day In Camden
Shirley Bunyan
United Kingdom

1.

One Day In Camden
A greasy-spoon cafe on a Camden-grey day. I was tired,
hung-over, gut-shocked when I saw you
sipping coffee; black, no sugar.

Your face held a history that I wasn't part of. The sadness I
felt didn't make any sense.
Fried egg and bacon, half-eaten, redundant, lay dead on my
plate. I sipped tea in defence
as you noticed me looking. Eyes quickly averted, too late, I
was filigree falling apart.

You headed toward me in monochrome motion, your
flickering smile an abuse of the heart
"Hello" *'Do I walk or respond? Hell, you're scrap from the
past'.*

"Good to see you." *'Stay calm now. Pretend'.* "You, too. How
you doing?"

*'You have all the power. Don't hurt me. It's started, but how
will it end'?*

You smelled so familiar, of teen-aged nostalgia. Oppressive,
like Eastwood. A déjà vu crime.
Your hair (was it blacker?) a family of Ravens sat easy on
shoulders I'd thought of as mine.

Brain battled logic with wild insanity. Whimsical endings are celluloid parcels. Director's vanity,
wound up, rounded down. tied up with a bow. No ominous shadows,
no staring at stars too distant to grasp, or delicate rainbows too fleeting to last.

'Run. Don't look back' I was mush. 'Could you tell? Did you know? Could you see in my eyes
that I'm gasping and choking still under your spell'?

"It's been a long time." Your voice was the same. And the lips. Oh, the lips. The kisses I knew.
'Damn you. CLICHÉ me...' lips that could melt virgin snow in Siberia.
Same lips saying now with a smile, "Missed you." "Yeah?"
I replied in a desperate bid to stay light. Indifference is hard when your head's on the wall.

"You look good," you persisted. I held my composure (I think), though I shrunk to the size of a ball.
"Thanks," I shot back with a shrug. *'Coco diva'.*

'Why now? I was healing and reeling in plenty of frogs'

Your face, animated, invaded my psyche. Faint, faraway words in a vague monologue.
Mingled images sparked, neon-dark, unrelenting.
The battered Toyota head-rushed to the coast. Writhing fire-naked nights, waking tight

2.

to the memories still fresh in our sweat

"How's your wife?" And it wasn't a question so much as a canvas to paint with your mouth.
"What choice did I have. She was having a kid" You seemed suddenly weak. Were you clawing me in?

"He got sick last September. Didn't make it." *'Oh, God! What a slap. Did I want to know more'?*
"I'm sorry." *Well, what else could I say? Was I sorry? Of course. Very sorry. Who for?*

And then shame, in its torrents, smashed my heart. My pain was my pain. Your hurting was more.
Do I reach for that tear dripping soft on your cheek? Do I catch it or let it drop wet the floor?

Two isles in the ocean, connected beneath.
'Are the stepping stones there? Is the water too deep? Am I reaching for rainbows and drowning again?'

We sat with our thoughts to the drear of the rain
in a greasy-spoon cafe on a Camden-grey day.
The past is a murderer needing a rope.
A battered Toyota parked minutes away.
The future, a glorious, hazardous hope.

Magdalena
Jeanette Burney
United States

> "... and standing behind him at his feet, weeping, she began to wet his feet with her tears, and wiped them with the hair of her head, and kissed his feet, and anointed them with the ointment." –Luke 7:38

Magdalena, now I know what falling is—
the easy part is hair become the wind.
The choice is sneaking up to some dark room away
from clatter of emotion not yet named.
    Could it be that all my education was
    a preparation for the pleasure of the fall?
Once framed inside a window, I look down
and see each tiny speckle in the grass, the tiny lights
that do not wait or watch or care to call
    me down. I have known buildings underneath my feet—
    the soft old reticence of balconies and awnings,
their betrayals of the children who have leaned too far
for gravity, their musings on a day like this
quite stopped when feet hit first. No, windows mean
    displacement: light inside, so something must go out.
    Blest be the instinct to survive, and also blest
is whatever it is that travels. And so it is
that thought accelerates into emotion. Now:
to take a chance cannot be accident.

 And you took yours, my lady, falling on your knees
  to see a tiny sparkle in the grass, in him
who pulled you in and out of your identity.
The perfume was pure motion. And the light, the light
became you both, between the roof and floor.
 The easy part was after you made your hair a wing,
  and flew the distance down until your fingers found it,
found the bottom. Broken feathers at the neck,
those fingers lost, the feathers lifted with a breeze,
they lift and move, at random, far away.

Scattering your ashes
RICHARD BURTLE
United Kingdom

Beside the path, with freshly peppered dew,
(Clumsy consignment – I could hardly see)
Speedwell, dead-nettle, campion and you.

You walked the dogs here all the autumn through:
They're with me now - as usual straining to be free
Beside the path, with freshly peppered dew.

Then winter came, our apprehension grew
But you weren't ever "What will be will be",
Speedwell, dead-nettle, campion and you.

As I came in, kicked off my sodden shoe,
You asked about your favourite gnarly tree
Beside the path, with freshly peppered dew.

And I misled you, simply couldn't tell it true –
That storms had felled it late in January.
Speedwell, dead-nettle, campion and you:

I leave you all beneath a blinding blue,
Today's farewell to be reprised repeatedly
Beside the path, with freshly peppered dew,
Speedwell, dead-nettle, campion and you.

Catalina's Cattle
Jonathan Cant
Australia

SEPTEMBER Twenty-Eight in Forty-Eight.

   A Catalina tale I wish to tell—

her flight to Lord Howe Island and her fate.

Her mission from the mainland started well.

   She reached the isle—her designated place—

then turned for home but set a course to Hell;

when twenty minutes back towards the base,

   inside the cabin, petrol vapours reeked.

The crew knew then the challenge they would face.

The luckless seaplane's precious fuel now leaked,

   so she returned to reach the still lagoon

beneath the mist through which the mountains peeked.

As Angel Terns soared high towards the moon

   —above the Norfolk pines to where they flock—

the Air Force airboat powered down too soon.

Her fuselage would clip the ridge of rock,

   and on a field her fiery wreckage spread.

Lord, how she fell—a monumental shock!

Her grassy grave, a paddock for a bed.

   Her engines now no longer hum nor sing.

Flight's Golden Age lives only in our heads.

Heroic locals tended everything.

   The toll: two airmen lived and seven dead.

Now cattle graze around her broken wing.

Darius on the Underground
Alan Coombe
United Kingdom

His words cut our silence, and silent we sank in our seats,
heads bent to our books and screens, to make no threat: we travelled
the deep tunnels, through London's clay. We were solitary,
even those together, whose eyes met before their heads turned
to glance at his reflection in the dark carriage-window,
watching unwatched like Perseus did Medusa, fearfully.

We thought him 'mad', this new traveller, stentor, orator:
ill, victim to those states of mind that make some people shout.
The learned could diagnose, but had no less discomfort.
We guessed at a grievance, official's or lover's misdeeds,
not of the marvelous tales from those times so long ago,
that goldsmiths and potters reveal, and epic poets tell.

He told of Darius; how his steed had greeted the dawn,
to proclaim him King.[1] Of Sardig's gold and Egypt's silver,
defended along the royal road to Susa. Parthian,
Ethiopian crossing Hemalya. Ionian
spies on Indus. His army camped by Volga, confronting

---

[1] According to Herodotus, six nobles decided upon the monarchy of Persia through a test: the first whose horse greeted the sunrise would take the throne. Darius won, through deception – his slave, Oebares, rubbed his hand upon the genitals of a mare, before stroking the steed's muzzle, effecting a keen response.

Scythians - nomads, who declined the fight. [We shared a smile.]

There's no land, he declared, nomads need defend, nor conquer:
no distant nor uncharted place far beyond the Great Steppe,
their burial place. We lifted our heads to hear these tales.
How Darius struck Nidinta-Bel; Babylon was his.
Of Bactria, and gifts of the god Ahur Amazda.
We, the passengers, listened: an audience for a bard.

Warnham Pond
Alan Coombe
United Kingdom

Things start in their return; his father knew
Christ crucified, pinned to the Study wall.
Alchemists haunted the Nursery shelves,
spoken of late at night in cobwebbed rooms,
stories first nursed in a soft Sussex burr,
schooled to terror, in Latin and in Greek,
by clergymen and scholars. Great monsters
lived in Warnham Pond. The children knew one.

A lawn, siskin green, ran from Nursery
to School, ghosting nightshade to lost hamlets,
razed to improve the view. Before his rage
he'd hid mid rhododendron roots, to read;
nearby, redwoods buttressed his hermit's cell.
He folded his fears into paper boats,
clasped them close, ran fast past a portico,
its façade reflected in Warnham pond.

The father cocked a shotgun, confident,
scanned nearby reeds for skulking snipe, servants
flushed to zigzag flight. His son, first-born, wept,
screamed, set afire his boats, on Warnham pond.
And exile was born, comet-trailed, to seek,
to free, all living tenants of the tomb
from the masque of murderous landlords' crimes,
and history's mitred and red-capped lies.

Goshawk-eyed, he flew, above silted psalms,
decried consolations sung just for kings,
priests' offerings; ripped, damned, in volcanic
versified revolt, till a first skylark's
towering song impelled a humbler hymn.
He returned to a bridge by Warnham pond,
skimmed stones to reflections of home and cell,
which trembled, less clear, to a softer view.

Creole Wedding
Jean Cooper Moran
United Kingdom

Man, why you go to her, and not choose I?
My skin so soft and black as rarest pearl,
I am your knife-winged angel, swift to fly.
Don't turn away and choose that giggling girl.

She flirt, she dance, she blind you with a smile.
She lure you like a fisherman a fish.
I curse her, flood her sleep with everything that's vile
To steal your blackened heart, my only wish.

Half-hid in swampy shadows, like a spy,
I watch you on your Creole wedding day.
We are dark night demons, you and I.
Aren't you afraid of all that I might say?

I know the echoes of your empty soul.
These ghoul-grim secrets fast within my breast
Will help my angry heart achieve its goal.
If I succeed, the devil takes the rest.

Don't laugh at me, heart-hollow, cast aside.
Poverty chains me but I'm rich in hate
So, hear my gift to your mulatto bride.
I will be there, come early or come late.

I'll rip apart your half-wit's married life,
Pour acid truths upon your wedded wife.

(This revenge poem is a fictionalised account of the reason Mrs Rochester's first wife in 'Jane Eyre' was driven to madness. The inspiration comes from Jean Rhys's novel 'Wide Sargasso Sea').

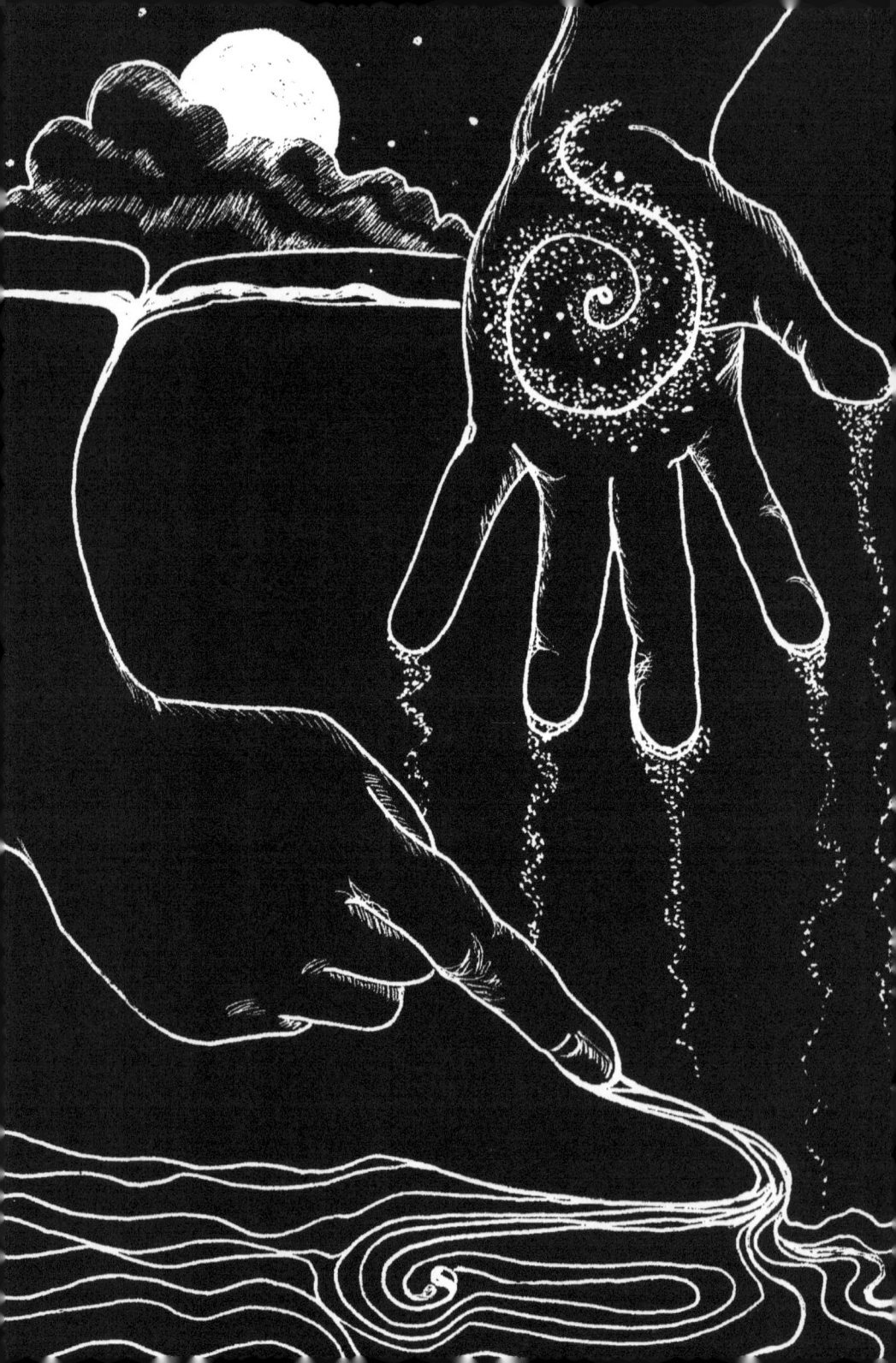

If the night had hands
Grace Copeland
United Kingdom

They'd be ageless. Roguish, nimble, taut with chalky scars, speckled silver. Palms like galaxies. Blood running like a cold tap, like brown ale in the promenade bars. They'd reach across the groaning belly of the sea with oiled fingertips. Slick her wind-chapped skin, draw unseen circles in the sand beneath and pick like breathlessness through wrecks she keeps, in search of fallen stars. As for you and me, a silk scarf tied across the eyes. If the night had hands they would be ours, smearing our thumbs along the coaly horizon, getting its dust all over our cuffs. Bringing blindness to every knife fight in a plastic bag. Clutching at air, never missing. Snuffing flames. If the night had hands, their lifelines would be broken in the middle. I've seen them before, risking everything, clutching the reins of a chariot. On the arms of

Nyx riding the painted lip of the world. Gold like the heat of a good dream. I've seen them push the dawn out from the water. If the night had hands, they'd be a mother's. They'd pinch our cheeks. Sprinkle sleep on the sleepless. They'd draw a curtain over Penshaw Folly, Fullwell Mill. Make the shape of prayer for all the boys who scarper to the shore to bathe their bloodied lugs in briny quiet. Throw a blanket over all the wayward girls.

stopping the bleeding
Lucy Crispin
United Kingdom

I had nosebleeds all the time when I was little:
the pillow cold and claggy with blood when I woke,
my mouth rank with the emetic iron tang.
I'd clamp cold-soaked loo roll to the bridge of my nose
or stuff it with rough, torn-off, suffocating plumes.
The great scarlet gouts had a mesmerising beauty
splatting rhythmically, not-quite-noiselessly, onto pale
porcelain.
Water went pink as it whisked the blood away,
the tap's whistle loud in the silent house.

When it finally stopped, knowing I mustn't wake them
(we've got Work in the morning) I'd stand by their bed,
miserable with hope, watching them breathe;
landing light slanted thin and yellow
across their present-but-absent, huddled forms.
When I got too cold I'd go back to bed
and remind myself of Grandpa: how he'd whistle for the cat
which from streets away would bound to greet him—

drape all day round his shoulders, like furs on a king;
how at their house he'd hold a sheet of *The P and J*
to draw the fire, or bring me hot Bon Accord lemonade in bed.
Setting down the mug, he'd turn at the door.
*Now then, dearie, if ye're needin' onything durin' night-time,
just call me.* But I always slept through.

My sister and I were horrible to him sometimes,
putting make-up on him while he slept, or Granny's curlers
in his sparse grey pelmet of hair. Once we made him tea
with every herb in Mum's rack (*it tasted affy, Nora,
but I had to drink it: the quinies made it*).
Thank god, then, that I also remember the slap of feet,
me running all the way down Clifton Road to Foresterhill
to hold his stroke-clenched hand with its thickened nails.
It was chill under my warm one. I couldn't soothe it
into straightness, but thank god I tried.

Nostalgia is the Devil
GILLIAN D'SOUZA
Germany

Good health's a funny thing.
People wish her well, and
laud her wellbeing at 95.
my begrudging smile,
now a mere disguise
for things they do not know,
for this pain we gatekeep,
behind old, decrepit doors.
All these sleepless nights,
moments rare when she
remembers me.

Incessant wailing, hysteria.
Her nails break into my skin,
a new realization dawns,
that we'll ever be bound:
her fading mind, my guilt.
Fragments of my grandma,
that I cling to with gloom
some days I'm her mother,

or her sister, learning new tunes.
I don all these hats, hopeless:
that one day I'll forget her too.

Nostalgia is the devil.
It is truly wearying how
my parents will debate
daily over a sleeping pill:
"Let her age without burden
before life sets her still."
Is it peace over morality?
Why must we dare choose?
Poor gran can't see nor hear.
She only suffers and wails,
while we hold on to nostalgia.

Shortlisted in the Poetry Category

The Opening
Hallie Denison
United States

> "Perhaps Truth is like the woman who will not be won."
> – Nietsche

The opening,
that nameless woman that we follow,
is only a mistake:
A bird dropped out of branches drawn
on soundless canvas
like the sky—
his falling out
will cause him to remember how
to fly.

It is not a tunnel
seen inside, and dark, that opens
on a small round landscape, growing
larger with the approach;
not even like
the lilies on the lake
that open to possess the air
or be possessed;
but

a random
route of travel chosen
by a pair of fated eyes—he's winging
up over trees and roofs
of houses in the city, alerted
to the dust and rain in open
spaces—

It is periphery in vision
that keeps him
from the near collision;
and it's the chance for accident
that causes plan and order:
opening
the unseen eye
that looks
onto a landscape full
of obstacles, and knows
a flying pattern
that it cannot name.

An ill-fitting dress of somebody else's design
Steven Duggan
Ireland

A girl, on a day not of her choosing,
is handed a dress made by others
which disregards her tastes or preferences,
her likes and dislikes,
her freedoms of movement and of thought.
Weighted with it, sewn into it, denied any other but
the one that's laughed at,
the one that's leered at,
the one left in tatters through desperate attempts at alteration.
The one judged in mirrors, and meetings, and bedrooms.
The one which wears and unravels.
The one which is creased, patched and torn.

And is told once again the old lie:
You'll grow into it.

Supermarketsweep
Steven Duggan
Ireland

I don't believe in love

although like all faiths
I know that one too can return

(before firing squads
on falling planes
or cast adrift at sea)

I'm agnostic not atheist then
ill equipped for philosophical or theological disputes -
knowing only that when I look to the heavens
I see no alignment in the stars

(or at least none concerning me)
and if I spy someone passing in the aisles
I know they will see right through me

(in both senses of that phrase)
and I will stir no pious ecstasy

before they reach for their pasta or beans.

SHORTLISTED IN THE POETRY CATEGORY

Rare beauty
Kate Durrant
Ireland

It's a thing of rare beauty the all-inclusive buffet.
A never ending wave of congealing calories that undulates across acres of stainless steel, so highly polished that you can see your bloated all-inclusive face in its shiny skin.
Waitresses hover like walking condiments as bright orange grated carrot fights rind-off cucumber and vibrant red beetroot for attention,
the long line of cheap fillers, decoys to distract you before you reach the excitement of the plat du jour.
Young couples, fresh from morning foreplay of pool keepy-uppy, pile their plates,
eyes eating only each other, stripped of sauce, dressings and artificial additives,
glowing with the all-inclusive sex of their first holiday.
So much love.
So much coleslaw.
The hungry queue outside the landlocked 'Ocean View' restaurant displaying their wrist bands of entitlement.
some dressed for dinner, some for each other, some for the 1990's.
Protein-powder-puffed men wearing tightly fitted Hugo Boss t-shirts eat with Keto restraint, as their stick-thin

girlfriends delicately nibble chips with their whitened teeth, and children in plastic high chairs smile disarmingly, trying to catch the eye of someone, anyone, who will break the tedium with a game of napkin peekaboo.
Tattoos stretch as plates empty, bicep-adorning ink etched faces of loved ones distorting and growing chins, incidental all-inclusive victims too.
Photographs are taken on omnipresent phones that never leave restless hands,
'making memories' as the diners fight to live firmly in the past or the future,
anywhere but here, anytime but now.
Slippery spaghetti and clandestine conversation spill over from table to table.
'I never wanted three,' she says, spearing vivid green broccoli dripping with garlic oil slowly and sadly into her unhappy mouth,
you listen, and hope she is talking about her dogs and not her children.
My love of many years sits patiently across the white-clothed table, his dimmed eyes starring inward at the blank gallery of his mind where once our portraits hung.

'A bit of everything?' I ask and he nods in acquiescence, not understanding but trusting me nonetheless.
I dart from bain marie to hot plate returning with an accountants-size inexpensive stoneware dish hidden under a rainbow of lurid green jelly, synthetic-cream topped sponge, and the devilishly hard to plate creme caramel.
He smiles and takes up his spoon, his eyes lighting up as the feast in front of him dims the noise of the insatiably hungry that surround us.
I push the empty plate in front of me to one side as I watch him eat,
saving my calories for the alcohol needed to dull the reality of the last chance buffet.
Beautiful.

SHORTLISTED IN THE POETRY CATEGORY

Cauldron, Star
ELIA ELTON
Australia

The Soul that rises with us, our life's Star,
Hath had elsewhere its setting,
…
trailing clouds of glory do we come. (W. Wordsworth)

Children we are, in the hands of guides,
forming in the image.
Cracking with the knife,
bathing **in** cauldron, brewing to honey.
What sun-warmed stones to lie on,
curling and twining, weaving into existence.
To wake from sleep and forgetting, not naked but clothed
in textured life.
Travelling from the east, from 'nature's priest',
chasing heaven from beginning to beginning.
The vision of the **rose-touched** sunrise,
the Sufi banquet, the flame-fed poetry -
the tapestry of the soul in 'common day',
the firmament of life's star.

The Chthonic Switchboard Blues

Deborah Finding
United Kingdom

Good morning, how may I direct your call?
Yes sorry, the signal here's not that great.
Hades? He called for you? Oh I see, bad luck,
I mean, I'll buzz you down. Have a good day!

How was your night? Long and dark, wasn't it?
I could have slept for eternity without the alarm.

Good morning, how may I direct your call?
Persephone? She's only here part-time,
let me check. Ok, yes, this is one of her months.
Putting you through. Don't mind the crying!

Do you want half this pomegranate? Go on.
I should stop snacking before lunch! Save me.

Good morning, how may I direct your call?
Charon? He's out on the boat right now,
can I take a message to pass on for him?
Pick up at four, Styx, no problem. Thanks.

I hate taking these oversubscribed bookings!
But I suppose it doesn't matter if it capsizes...

Good morning, how may I direct your call?
God? Sorry, there's no one of that name here.
Wait! Checking, I see he is onboarded to start -
could you call back in seven hundred years?

Another intern! Wonder how long this one will last.
Still, couldn't make things any worse though, eh?!

American Psycho
Jacqueline Gamboa
United States

I'm a wet dream
The girl next door
With a mean streak
Miss America as a whore

You'll chase me down
Until you have a tight grip
You'll take my crown,
My body, and my lips

You'll think that you own me
Like every man before you
Until I become a bit unruly
And you won't know what to do

You'll start off with the usual
Say I'm crazy and unstable
That I must be delusional
They always start with the labels

You'll try your best to walk away
Dodge me like a bullet
And hate me at the end of the day
Spit in my face, tell me I deserved it

Everyone loves to hate a woman
Because it could never have been him
She must be the problem
Eve, after all, was the original sin

But if I dressed for success
Like your beloved Patrick batman
Would you still see me as less?
Or could I be the protagonist then?

Why do we as a society
Accept men's outbursts and rage
But only want women in piety
Keep them locked in their cage

What if I became the next American Psycho?
Would you send me love letters in prison
Beg for me to be let go
Tell them I should be forgiven?

Or would you stand by and watch
Wait for my trial date
Get out the popcorn and your best scotch
Because they love to watch us burn at the stake

Phone Call
Jennifer Harrison
Australia

          It's possible to destroy the ones
     you love on the phone
even when you don't
      mean to offend anyone   it might be

         a problem of family attitude
     the way farmers learn to wire their emotions shut
never hot or cold   neither shouting at mishap
      nor overexcited by a dump of rain –

         it's like there's a family boardgame
   just for us
a toy railroad that runs beside
      a miniature town   the baby doll in bed

         the woman at her vanity   the man
    outside in his woodpile with an axe
the kitchen table set with roses   a tiny takeaway
      box of chicken nuggets on a white plate

     the toilet seat up or down . . .
   meanwhile the old train runs on time
the carriages scarcely lurching
    newspapers tidily spread open

     at the correct page
   sport births/deaths it depends . . .
each hour lived as though it's ordinary
    each morning never really goes away

     time is already in the past
  or neatly paused –
it's possible to sweep a family of wooden pegs
    down the telephone

     when you say
    I don't believe in god anymore
the little birds have left the fence near the Irish dry-stone
wall
    can't we be different today?

The Idea Of It
Amanda Huggins
United Kingdom

In his unexpected late night text,
he suggests a drink
– maybe this week or next?
Take a chance on us, Molly, he says.

And you're already recalling that basement bar,
the press and jut of groin and hip
on a crowded Dalston dance floor,
the fullness of his bottom lip,
the graze of teeth on skin,
that rhythmic push against a cold white wall,
the hurl and reel and blur and spin.
And you relived every moment
on the last bus home:
the surprise taste of you on his tongue,
that token wave of shame
before all the rush and yell and spill of him
crashing in. Then your number on his hand
and his on yours; that written promise of so much more.

In his unexpected late night text
he suggests you meet for a drink sometime
– maybe this week or next?
Take a chance on us, Molly, he says.

But though it's what you thought you wanted,
you know there's not a chance you'll call,
because you can already see the scuffed blue walls
in a cheap hotel room on the fifteenth floor,
can already feel the slip and glide of skin on skin,
see the ravel of
mouths and limbs, hands pressed against the glass,
wanting the world to share
his thrust and spill and gasp.
And so, and so, you roll him once around your mouth
before typing no. You could bow to fate, but you need to
let go, because you think the idea of it – oh you *know*, you
know –
the idea of it is too perfect to ever risk letting it happen.

3rd Place in the Poetry Category

High Tide
Dave Kurley
Portugal

Maybe one too many caipirinhas
Maybe her mates thought it would be a hoot
To leave her, snoring and slavering,
In a cheap white plastic garden chair
Perched on the brow of the beach

Maybe the tide tickled her feet awake
And she jump-started
As the sea busily devoured the shore
Between her and her hotel
A meal it enjoyed every high tide

Maybe she would have tottered without the undertow
Heels in one hand -
And who wears heels in the sand?
Her handbag held high in the other

The walk back became a test
Of teeth gritted, of strength, of endurance
As each successive wave plucked and pulled at her
Every stumble, every sodden step, heavy and drenched

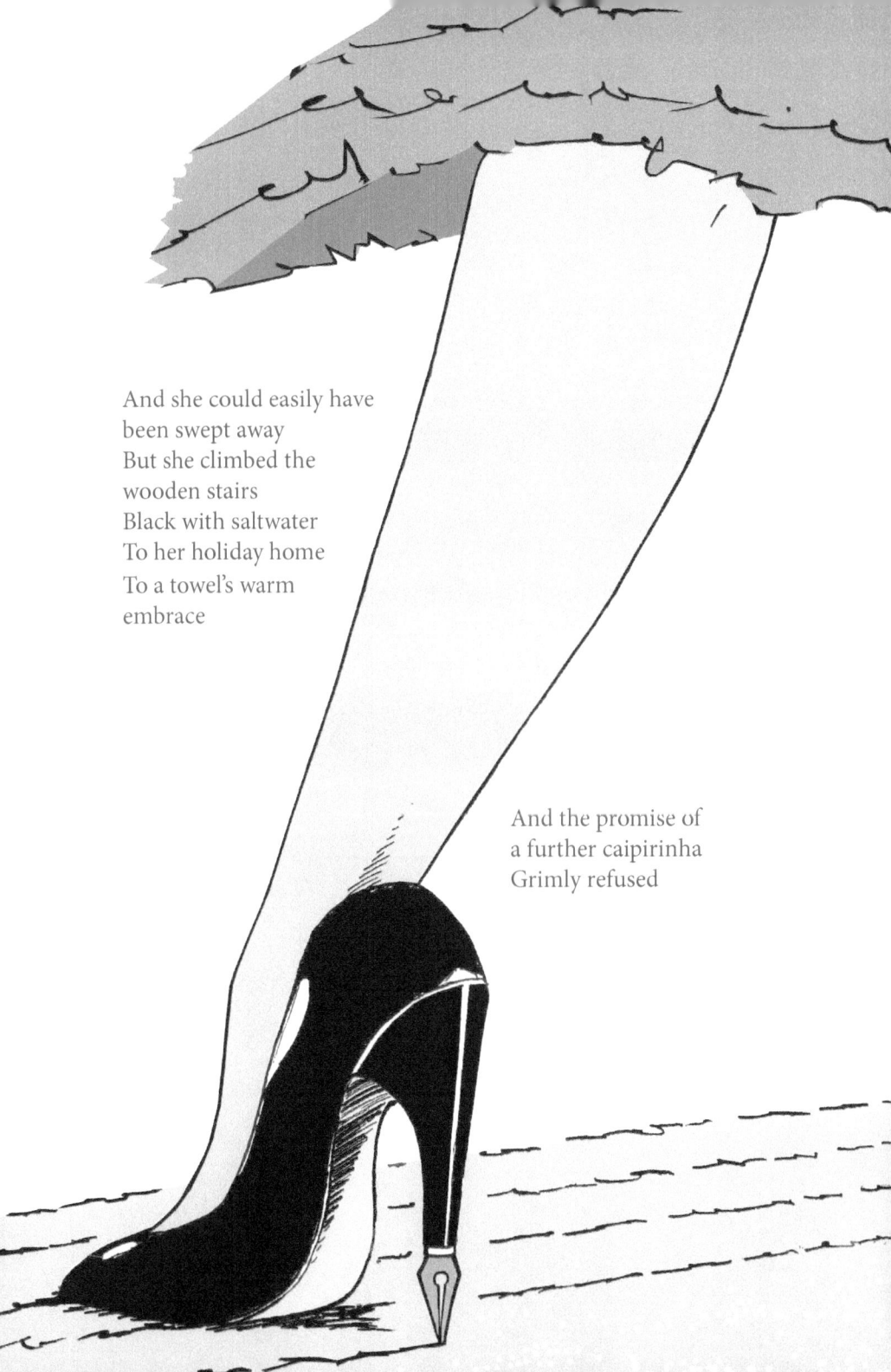

And she could easily have been swept away
But she climbed the wooden stairs
Black with saltwater
To her holiday home
To a towel's warm embrace

And the promise of a further caipirinha
Grimly refused

Washed Up
DONALD MCCRORY
Spain

(based on a true event witnessed in Thessalonika)

Distant daughter of Aphrodite
she met her death in her mother's womb.

No loved ones, relatives, friends or flowers
or a single sound of solemn music;
not one word from the Book of Psalms
or a tear to soften life's ultimate pain,
not even a name to fill a hurried prayer.

Colder than cathedral stone,
whiter than the sails of passing summer yachts,
she had been drifting – so they said –
since the early hours when the sea is warmer.

Fished out by impervious off-shore police,
she now laid sprawled across damp paving,
drowned in the waters she had known since birth.

Dead to our eyes that looked at her corpse,
to our minds that searched for motives, clues,
to hearts that felt the frailty of life,
her inert body, unblushingly bare,
lay steeped in stillness, the shroud of peace.

Lured by the sea's latest catch
onlookers stared in repeated silence,
until an ambulance appeared, as if in a film,
reminding us that routine ultimately prevails.
She was quickly covered and then conveyed
to the cold formality of the post-mortem,
the final abuse of her female form,
another entry in the coroner's report.

The Verdict
DONALD McCRORY
Spain

(From national newspaper reports)

Born in sin, unwanted since birth,
home life null and void. Sent to school
unloved. Clocked time in class and left when
legal. Joined the army, proved a man among men
in the SAS. Trained to keep his cool
under extremes. But came down to earth

with a bang when demobbed. Suffered years
of depression. He honestly didn't belong.
Became a regular in dole queues. Quick slide
to despair: no friends, money, purpose. Tried
to lead a 'normal' life. Then things 'went wrong'
last Summer; he shot a policeman then 'disappears'.

When on the loose he's savagely pursued
as if a terrorist and enemy of the State.
Vestiges of SAS training kick in; he retreats
Rambo-like, to moorland. A frightened farmer treats
him to a full farmhouse breakfast, although late.
He calls it "The Last Supper". Rued

the day he was born. His last words:
"You live in this world and no one
knows who you are". A lonely voice in East
Yorkshire not heard by marksmen or a priest
as twelve rounds (sic) are fired on the run.
But for what? At dawn two shots, like birds,

screech into the air. One hit
a tree, the other went through his head.
Both counted. Claimed he couldn't face thirty
years inside. So proud, unemployed, Willy
Pruden, real name Edwards, fell, filled with lead.
'A simple case of suicide', said the coroner. But was it?

SHORTLISTED IN THE POETRY CATEGORY

A Piece Of Glass
Donald McCrory
Spain

(Based on reports of midwives I met in rural India)

With hands and feet as hard as sun-baked soil,
India's peasant women, despite the heat
that penetrates their work-soiled saris,
will smile angelically
for tourists who have time, money and film to spare.

But come the time when birth is imminent
they carry, as their mothers did,
a piece of sharpened glass,
for in the field there is no mid-wife
or a passing para-medic. These girls have learnt
to cut the cord themselves.
That's why the glass is kept
so fine, so pure, and prized
as much as Krishna's shining face,
the one that brightens mud-brick walls
in town and village tea-shops.

When the crystal has done its baby work
the child is carried – doubly blessed if male –
back home to where her in-laws
wait with gifts of garlands and homemade treats.
Amid sweet smiles and songs
of praise, she quietly returns the polished
glass to grandma's shrivelled hand.
And so birth proceeds to birth,
without the use of scans,
 pre-natal exercises or
advice on vitamins or baby-foods.
A week or two of rest
then back to work, content to cut
the crop or sew new seed.

Stormcock Harbinger
ALISON MCNULTY
United Kingdom

> *Thrusshe sings the phrase 'Sanctus, Sanctus',*
> *from Renaissance poem, 'The Harmony of Birds.'*

The mistle thrush
          warns when storms will come
detecting the change.
              Before skies darken
he flutes his Sanctus
          from stirred treetop.
Day ends as dusk
          creeps in our garden
and skeleton leaves
          clatter the windows.

Listening I think,
          why does the stormcock
know trouble is near?
            Does he hear lightning's roar
feel wind's iced fingers
          sense the danger?
As he stands
          on mistletoe duty
gorging berries
          hurling rattles at crows,

I wonder if storm cock
                knows he's sowing
the seeds of his
                own destruction.
When he wipes sticky beak
                on oak tree wood,
when he excretes
            seeds on fertile ground
more birdlime is spread
                to stick his feet down

on hidden traps,
            whose signs can't be read.
Some of us, like the mistle thrush,
                spread warnings
ill-winds are coming.
            They flute their Sanctus
as our skies darken.

Paternoster Row - passing in green velvet jackets
GRAEME MILES
Australia

for Elia

I'm feeling traces of your old sadness –
love returned badly or not at all,
sly evasions of commitment covered
by a macho bluff. Without much use
I want to reach back to younger you,
brush away the careless, persistent flies.
I want the years on our way
to each other to be better.
                              I hope
when we lived in the same street
and didn't quite meet that we passed
and smiled for no clear reason,
each in the green velvet jacket
that we owned, had a moment sharing
that lush flourish of dress.

                                    But if
I could reach back to you
it might change as well the moments
we eventually met, the joyful shock
of thinking, 'there you are,
that's where you got to all this time.'

Forever Walk
Alan Mitchell
United Kingdom

I wish I hadn't seen him there
Beige blanket
Body still and cooling
All aspects of what made him
HIM gone

A scamp, a character
Fierce and fiercely loyal
He would jump so high when she came home
Waiting at the door as she drove through the gates
refusing to return when we're running so late
He had to come in so we could go!

yet these last nine months, a gift
(which, my daughter told me through tears, worryingly
that a person could have a baby during)
and all then fuelling sadness when
we knew, just today, it. was. time.

I stayed with my girl whilst wife went in
to hold and soothe last moments
as they dripped like broken tap
and his trusting face as they closed blue door

I should have remembered him like that, 'poorly'
(that indeterminate state medicals tell you on the phone)
but alive
when he'd gone and tears were falling
something from that sad room calling
and I answered

and saw sweet little dog, blank eyes open
seeing nothing now save
the long forever walk

I had to bite back bitterness
and tears, and be just then, strong

although my own heart broke

This Machine
ALAN MITCHELL
United Kingdom

my life is in those pills there
blistered packs of chemicals
to regulate this, counteract that
and basically, keep this sad machine running

not running well, you understand
nor in tip-top purring form
like a well-tuned race car
no
this rusty bucket that misfires
and has shoddy breaks and gears
can sometimes barely get going at all, and hills?
Lord knows are to be avoided!

my ritual?
why, I count out the pills
some chalky and some shiny
seated on my lonely bed with boxes
barricading in around me
I sit as if besieged by the call
of time, echoing with laughter

Small pills, small colour coded boxes
(they even note the names of the day to help me)
that for some reason I place an order and ready
weeks in advance
Yet
one day
one week
one month
some will rest in their boxes
unused
not needed
as this machine,
misfiring for the last time,
slowly
 breaks
  down

Rite of Passage
VAL ORMROD
United Kingdom

On the day that trust is forever shattered,
you lie, pinned by firm hands –
a stab of hope as you look for Mama.

You see the too-bright gleam of your sisters' eyes,
the splintered looks that jag between them.
But Mama would surely not hurt you.

They bring white paint to daub your face,
animal skins to swathe your young shoulders,
Mama's beaded collar for your neck.

The pain will make you strong, little sister,
it's what your future husband will expect.
But Mama will surely not hurt you.

Your skirt pushed up, legs prised apart,
splayed on the hard, parched earth.
Surely Mama will never hurt you.

But it is Mama who brings the razor
as she refuses to meet your eyes,
Mama who nods assent to the Elder

for the slicing through of your innocence,
as you scream and go on screaming,
Mama who stands proud by the lake of blood.

Shortlisted in the Poetry Category

When Cassandra Stumbles
Miranda Pratt
United States

A crystal ball shatters on the blacktop,
leaving shards of prophecy to glisten
like freshly fallen snow beneath our boots.

Crushed with every backward step, they lose
their bite, receding into abstract doom:
Setting suns. Smoldering hills. Falling ash.

We reap and sow and reap again. Charting
disembodied dreams of present perfect,
stretched clear beneath annihilation skies.

Her eyes turn red with future strain. Mine,
with looming failure as sea levels kiss
my throat and drag me down by the ankles.

Nothing soothes the horror of a finished
story save for spilling ink over *The
End*. And so, I reach for violet, crossing

out our epilogue in frantic pen strokes.
Shrouding my heart with plastic to keep the
dust at bay, I set out on the highway,

seeking revelation. It glitters in
a bank of frozen memory. Relieved,
I sweep it into piles. Then, reach for glue.

A Writer's Fate
Jean Rafferty
United Kingdom

We were on a journey, an exploration,
requiring the skills of thinker and warrior.
Some thought me gothic, strange.
Maybe… I craved purple velvet,
black lace, dark red roses.

We crossed borders, raging torrents,
vertiginous cliffs where we plunged downwards,
only to swoop back up on eagles'
wings. We subverted rules, challenged
guards, bent time and space to our will.
But still we were left with questions…

Through the dark a small figure
emerged, a tiny red peacock,
hopping from one place to another,
its jewelled tail winking as it roamed.
Where did it come from? Nonchalant,
it fluttered to a halt and unfurled
its dazzling panoply of gems.

Sad Outcomes
GABHAINN RITCHIE
United Kingdom

There seemed dark faces in the trees
by the car park at the parlour.

We hadn't yet gone in, for grandfather's superstition
promised sad outcomes if we did

and if his casket was open
to the waxy, beige sepulchral ceiling.

His fierce dead face will have to stare
at his stareless drooping lids;

My brother, braver than I, tried to pry
them open. They wouldn't.

We hope he sees his deeds in life and sights
just how he loved to hold our gran

by her twig thin wrists and watch her
weep her weeping.

The Lonely Prince
Angel Rodriguez
United States

Off Beat Poetry

I can fall to the depths of my Hell
I cannot fly into the heavens quickly enough
But even then, Heaven or Hell won't accept me

I'm always anxious
I'm never fine
I'm afraid of death
Though not afraid to die for another

When I bind my wings to swallow its sin
Ivory escapes from my pores, quartz digs into my skin
Heaven and Hell have been forever against me

Deny yourself saviour and open arms from The Father
An apple falls
A snake is lost
Alas I taste the sand

Fall to the depths of my Hell, and soon you will see
That Heaven releases the demons trapped within me

WINNER IN THE ORIGINS COMPETITION

Ma Mer, Maman
PARIS ROSEMONT
Australia

I find myself

    here   again

        by the foaming mouth   of the sea, listening

to her indecipherable whispers

            shhhh…..   shhhh…..

                          it's going to be okay

I come here

    in times of distress

                  she comforts me

        more than my cold birth

      mother ever could

I nestle into the Oedipal womb of my longing

    as she strokes my hair, silken as seaweed singing lullabies:

hush, hush my darling—

        come suckle in the wet of our mutual wanting

                and I shall cradle you

                      till my bed runs dry

Pleading
Paula Rowlands
Australia

She asked the universe to bring her a change
to get her away from the cruel and strange
at night she'd dream and wish upon stars
never going out or near any bars
handing to the universe all that she feels
in the hope that her soul finally heals

She'd lay and wonder why she got a raw deal
it's not like she was lacking in sex appeal
a beautiful soul and a pretty face
pleading to the cosmos to find her a place
to get her away from the things that hurt
before her body was covered in dirt

Pleading, wishing, hoping in the night
for a little more magic to make her days bright
the days were full of grey and blue
but oh she'd wished for colourful hue
she cried again 'This can't be my fate
I clean I scrub, I'm never late'

She deserved much more than the hand she'd been dealt
The stones were cast and on the ground she knelt
What would they reveal, would her wishes come true
Was the cosmos listening? She had no clue
The very next morning while scrubbing the floor
Fate stepped in with a knock at the door.

A Kismet Path
Mervyn Seivwright
Germany

your birthplace is not forecasted
your chess-piece is not prescribed

nor the social class
nor the family name
nor the fiscal fate

when the womb spawned you
no overview script bestowed
of the village   city   region   country

where scrawling warlords erase the canvas
city slums   communes of salvage-home cages
one-traffic-light towns   sloughing in degradation

a harvest to manifest
predestinate men   unleashing their wrath
the uneasy sounds   resonating

a mother's hum
followed by wall-shakes
buckling metal melting

blazed sun colors after a lightning thunderclap
whisking-wind hiss   fiery flush
scattering your mother's steps

your smells of familiarity   sunflower fields
vanishes   fleeing   whether you are
a child   teen   adult   off the road

your shoes scuffle   tearing apart   over kilometers
tromping across terrain   floating on rubber rafts
repulsed by your "refugee" name

if you escape   you promise yourself
to chisel your chess-piece   in prized position
planted on a board   not burning

Conkers
Lee Slingsby
United Kingdom

"You're obsessed with conkers."
It was true, at sixty years old, I still was.
I knew why I loved conkers so much.
They transported me to my childhood,
A time of no expectations,
No worries, no fears.
But most of all they took me to my brother.

High-pressure days, swimming pool skies.
No cotton wool clouds in sight.
Nothing to spoil the azure,
To detract from the depth.
"It feels like we're running off the edge of the world,"
As we ran towards the conker-laden trees.
"We're explorers, aren't we?"

That's what he said,
I believed him, and I still do.
Because when the wind rustles,
Through the horse chestnut trees,
I hear his voice.
When I see the endless blue,
And I know he's watching me.

When I hear my granddaughter laugh and giggle,
I see his face contort with laughter.

Not as I saw him on the day he died,
I see that brown-eyed little boy.
Worry-free, without his ghosts and demons,
That chased him through a fragmented life.
And in that moment, I love him with all my heart.
Conkers are bulging in his pockets,
A smile spreads across his face,
And on my dark cold nights,
This image keeps me warm and safe.
Then my thoughts turn to our mother,
Holding my younger brother in her arms,
Stroking his head and ruffling his hair.

Her compassion, her understanding,
Comforts me even now, years later.
It brings me succour,
Through the first fall of conkers.
If it didn't,
The conkers would take away my mind,
And they were never meant to do that.

Because they were put on earth,
To bring screams and giggling excitement.
In an Autumn spectacular,
Residing in a mile-high amphitheatre.
Before the harshness of Winter arrives.
Conker season a last gentle reminder,
Of a Summer that's slowly fading away.

I know you're all with me,
As I commit this memory to paper.
Mum, Dad but most of all you Steven.
Forgive me, brother,
I took all the big conkers before you had a chance,

You know how greedy I am,
I loved those brown diamonds.

"Have you got enough," he'd shout.
"My pockets are full."
We'd then make our way out of the park as dusk approached.
Because goblins and ghouls,
Reside in conker trees at night,
They dislike little boys,
Taking away their treasure.

Back home, in front of the fire.
The spoils would empty onto the floor.
Our favourite part,
The counting and the sharing,
Of the big un's and the little un's.
"We've got to have the same size conkers, it's important, Martyn."
And it was, when nothing else mattered.

Peregrine
Simon Tindale
United Kingdom

climbed the stone steps
wondering why he'd
never made it to the top

of the class at school
or his job at the museum
or the ornithological society

who'd finally agreed
to let him talk
about The Imperious Falcon

which circled overhead
but as he perched on the edge
of Malham Cove, he twitched

and fell.

The bird pecked at his remains
which is all he ever wanted,
someone to pick his brains.

Bathing the Tyrant
Glen Wilson
United Kingdom

Where gooseflesh meets goosebumps,
hair recedes to ancestral borders,

one that once splashed through the Volga,
shivers in his bare chest.

I slowly sponge the sores
that used to make him flinch,

but they are so many, the puckered skin
calmed only by over-prescription.

Still even a weak creature can train a bear to dance
if he is given the whip and the cub early enough.

Where minutes before steam rose with such heat,
ripples only a tepid body of water,

the limbs shorten as they strain upwards,
by a rifle's prompting, I look away.

Like beads of a prayer chotki the plug chain
rattles against enamel and iron

as the scum and water empties,
the plughole gurgles,

almost like applause.

They Will be Winged
Raya Yarbrough
United States

I don't know what this time in the world is.
It's dust off a cat's back and planets in foreign orbits.
It's all the palm print of the same God.
Or particulate God-ness
scattered from an original stone.

These are the years when we rioted for stillness.
When we cracked our knuckles
before we kneeled to pray.
When we put the magic in boxes, in attics, and in glove
compartments, and just fucking swallowed it
because we could be neither bothered
nor enchanted,
by the dreams of innocent days.

I don't know what time of the world this is, there's not
enough drink to kill this sober.
But I know we are the guardians of the world after now.
The world, blessed for them who follow,
who will thrive, for the passing of us.
And they will find the hidden treasures
of humanness, which we coveted,

like hatchlings,
untouched from the storm.

They will find the best we left.
And they will be winged.

Well Maybe, Anyway, This Was Destiny
Kathy Zwick
United Kingdom

In a burst of 1840s cooperation and community
forty sturdy local farmers' sons and their burly teams of horses
toiled long summer nights to dam the river and dig a tailrace.

A local grist mill - accessible and open to all.
A community landmark, a destination.

Exquisite stone-ground quality "Magnolia Flour"
crafted with love and care - the pride of the community.
Communal pride shared by all.

To prevent tainting of the precious grain
or any hint of racy rancid spoilage
the wheat germ was carefully, carefully ferreted out
and lovingly carried home each night.
Wives baked delicious, nutritious wheat germ muffins.

Grandpa George stood by the dam all night and watched.
That savage, callous, cruel night, 13 March 1920,
the burly rains pummelled - and they threatened.
The newly built concrete dam upstream
burst.

The Roaring Twenties came in with a rancorous roar.
Ice blocks and stocky concrete chunks cascaded
downstream -
rollicking and rowdy, crunching and destroying both dam
and mill -
and a whole community's pride and its history.
Henry Ford quickly bid and bought the site;
he quickly razed the beloved (now dilapidated) old mill.
A new car parts factory quickly mushroomed
for a bursting new infant enterprise.

Alas, one tried to hide communal tears
and to rationalise that, well maybe, anyway,
this was destiny -
those giant shiny new faster hot steel Minnesota rollers,
rollicking and rowdy, and the fictional Betty Crocker
were all racing to replace the gentlemanly old stone
grinders.

The beloved nutritional muffins were also destined for
decline.

SONGWRITING
Lyrics Category

1st Place in the Songwriting Category

The Cloak
Michael Pettit
South Africa

I'm in the song, cocooned in light
Out there, beyond its glow, there's night
Cool gloom, and gazes sunk in shade
Ghosts stare back at me, then fade

They come and go, dim phantoms swim
Then, like a bruise, he's there, it's him
Across a time, across a space
Across a void I touch his face

His shadow burns there in the dark
Soft flame can scar, love maps its mark
I skip a beat, reach out, he's gone
I look away, the song moves on

I take the song, I shape its line
And hold its hand and make it mine
I find a pulse, and make it real
And draw it round me, safe as steel

Don' wanna think, don' wanna feel
Don' wanna think, don' wanna ---

A flame, a ring, a stone, a sling
Turn your collar to the cold and sing
Forget that face, warm wounds won't heal
Let song lines weave a cloak of steel

What's dead can live, caress and cling
Its voice still cleave, its whisper sting
The night is long, I cut a deal
A tender song of tempered steel

Don' wanna think, don' wanna feel
Don' wanna think, don' wanna feel

Fate's hand is deft, it left no trace
Yet still I shelter from that face
And close a door, and set a seal
Cloak song around me, sure as steel

The night is cruel, it's cut is keen
I need this song, I trust it's sheen
A mesh of silks – don' wanna feel –
I sing a cloak that's sheer as steel
                as sheer as steel
           as steel
                  as sheer …
                        as steel

2ND PLACE IN THE SONGWRITING CATEGORY

Hey God, So What's The Hurry?
Jim Donaldson
United States

1. Up to now I've never been, the sort of guy who'll take a pen – and write a letter.
Tell you darlin' why it was, I couldn't help but fall in love – with you forever.
Maybe I've been too content, to ever think that I might spend – my life without you.
And now you lay there quietly, that's not the way it oughta be – and I start prayin'…

2. Amazed me how you wrestled life, somehow always won the fight – made things happen. And how you put a smilin' spin, on any news was lookin' grim – so's not to worry.
When drinkin' had the best of me, you said "make a choice, the booze or me"? That one was ez. And when we failed to make a babe, you had the will and found a way – they're here beside me.

Ch:
Hey, hey, hey there God, so what's the hurry? Seems to me you're preachin' to a full house. And though the choir may have an empty seat, still I'd be grateful if you'll leave - my darlin' here to sing - her lovin' song to me.

3. I've always been the sort of guy, looks a challenge in the eye - comes out swingin'.
But this one far as I can see, it's tougher than both you and me - got me worried.
And so tonight I'm writing you, to say the things I hope you knew - though I'm not certain. Wish we had more time to laugh, to say goodbye is so damn sad - and I start prayin'…

Bridge:
Cause if that's the way it's gonna be, then honey listen up to me. We'll be okay the kids and I. You go ahead and take your ride. We'll meet again - somewhere in Time.

Ch:
Hey, hey, hey there God, so what's the hurry? Seems to me you're preachin' to a full house. And though the choir may have an empty seat, still I'd be grateful if you'll leave - my darlin' here to sing - her lovin' song to me.

(Coda: Slow) Still, I'd be grateful if you'll leave - my darlin' here to sing - her lovin' song to me.

(Cold out)

3RD PLACE IN THE SONGWRITING CATEGORY

Over The Moon
PETER LUDGATE
United Kingdom

On a day in a land far away
By a stream in a place time forgot
With a smile and a wave of your hand
Told a tale of world now unknown

Somethings wrong with the air sang the birds
I can't breathe ,I can't see for the dust
And the leaves on the trees they are brown
At a time in the year they should be green

Look dead ahead ,at the incoming storm
Incoming storm outgoing life
Look at the ground,
at the brown at the brown
And say to yourself did we really do this ,did we really do this

Over the moon
The moon which reflects the earth which rejects
All that is true

When a man tells a lie to us all and
We believe what he says to the end
It's a shame no one checked thought again before
The weight of it all got to great
Just the birds who are left with a song
Its our time ,gone away,eaten up,
Am I dizzy am I done?
Is this the end of Summers run

I'm over the moon

SONGWRITING
Performed Song Category

1st Place
Back to Burscough
Elaine Ibiricu
United Kingdom

2nd Place
Salaam Shalom
Linda Barrett
United Kingdom

3rd Place
Prison Rain
Alan Mitchell
United Kingdom

Listen to the songs at:
www.hammondhouse.org.uk/music

Hammond House Publishing is a social enterprise and membership organisation founded by students at the *University Centre Grimsby* and run by volunteers. We aim to encourage and support creative talent in art and literature, providing opportunities for members to develop their skills, publish their work and follow a successful literary career.

Members benefit from reduced competition entry fees, author profile page, and the chance to participate in our range of cultural activities.

Our annual writing competitions and anthologies bring together some of the best writing talent from around the world. So far we have published over 200 writers from 28 countries.

Our literary activities support the work of other Hammond House organisations to address loneliness and isolation and promote positive mental health in both urban and rural communities.

www.hammondhouse.org.uk

Hammond House is a not-for-profit group of community organisations dedicated to supporting and encouraging creative people across all disciplines of arts and culture.

Our community outreach programmes contribute to easing loneliness and isolation, and promoting positive mental health.

Scan for the Hammond House Story

www.hammondhouse.org.uk

2023 International Literary Prize

The eighth year of our international literary prize saw a record number of entries spread across five continents.

Short Story

1st place: **It's Your Call, Baby!** Madeleine Armstrong, *UK*
2nd place: **Pigs & Paint,** Letty Butler, *UK*
3rd place: **Where My Body Meets The Water,** Christina Care, *UK*

Poetry

1st place: **The Purple Dress,** Vasiliki Albedo, *Greece*
2nd place: **If the night had hands**, Grace Copeland, *UK*
3rd place: **High Tide,** Dave Kurley, *Portugal*

Scriptwriting

1st place: **The Horsewoman,** Jessica Cotterill, *UK*
2nd place: **The Incident,** Elizabeth Carroll, *UK*
3rd place: **In or Out,** Nicky Denovan, *UK*

Songwriting (Lyrics Category)

1st place: **The Cloak,** Michael Pettit, *South Africa*
2nd place: **Hey God, So What's The Hurry?** Jim Donaldson, *USA*
3rd place: **Over The Moon,** Peter Ludgate, *UK*

Songwriting (Recorded Song Category)

1st place: **Back to Burscough,** Elaine Ibiricu, *UK*
2nd place: **Salaam Shalom,** Linda Barrett, *UK*
3rd place: **Prison Rain,** Alan Mitchell, *UK*

2023 INTERNATIONAL LITERARY PRIZE

The eighth year of our international literary prize saw a record number of entries spread across five continents.

2023 COMPETITION THEME SONG
Between The Lines

Written by Ted Stanley and performed by Green Dreaming

www.hammondhouse.org.uk

2024 INTERNATIONAL LITERARY PRIZE
Sponsored by the University Centre Grimsby and Royal Society of Art

Cash prizes and worldwide publication for all shortlisted entries.

THEME: **Time**

CATEGORIES:
Short Story
Poetry
Scripts
Performed songs
Song lyrics

Entries open on 22nd February 2024 and close on 30th September 2024

Full details and entry form on our website

www.hammondhouse.org.uk

The University Centre Grimsby, as part of the Grimsby Institute, is built on high expectations, a focus on learning, commitment to achievement and an engaged, practical education for all students.

A wide range of degree level courses are available including BA (hons) Creative and Professional Writing.

www.grimsby.ac.uk

www.ingramcontent.com/pod-product-compliance
Lightning Source LLC
Chambersburg PA
CBHW060616080526
44585CB00013B/857